◆ **Hispanic Headliners** ◆

Shakira

Star Singer

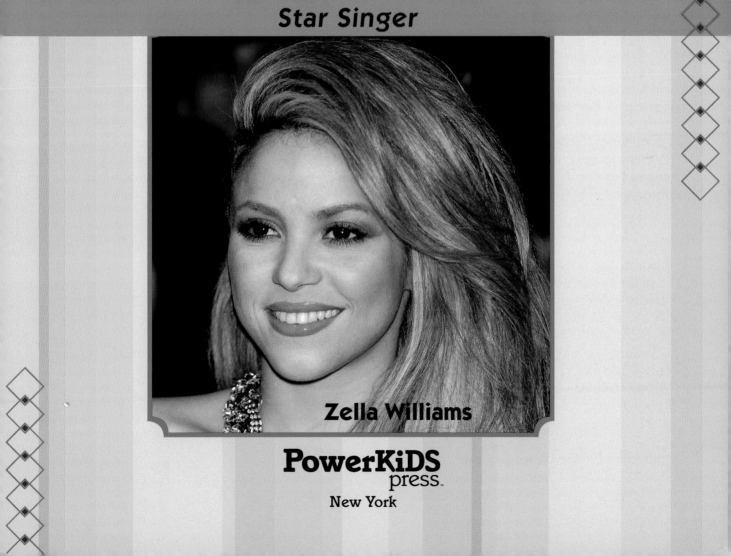

Zella Williams

PowerKiDS press.

New York

Published in 2011 by The Rosen Publishing Group, Inc.
29 East 21st Street, New York, NY 10010

First Edition

Editor: Joanne Randolph
Book Design: Kate Laczynski
Photo Researcher: Jessica Gerweck

Photo Credits: Cover, pp. 1, 6–7, 15 Carlos Alvarez/Getty Images; p. 4 Dave M. Benett/Getty Images; p. 5 Francisco Leong/AFP/Getty Images; p. 8 Bertrand Parres/AFP/Getty Images; p. 9 Jeff Kravitz/FilmMagic/Getty Images; p. 10–11 Damian Duncan/Sony Music Archive/Getty Images; p. 12 Scott Gries/Getty Images; p. 13 Alexander Hassenstein/Getty Images; p. 14 Ronaldo Schemidt/AFP/Getty Images; p. 16 AFP/Getty Images; p. 17 Timothy A. Clary/AFP/Getty Images; pp. 18, 19 Shehzad Noorani/UNICEF via Getty Images; p. 21 Fotonoticias/Wirelmage/Getty Images; p. 22 Juan Mabromata/AFP/Getty Images.

Library of Congress Cataloging-in-Publication Data
Williams, Zella.
  Shakira : star singer / Zella Williams.
     p. cm. — (Hispanic headliners)
  Includes index.
  ISBN 978-1-4488-1457-2 (library binding) — ISBN 978-1-4488-1480-0 (pbk.) — ISBN 978-1-4488-1481-7 (6-pack)
  1. Shakira—Juvenile literature. 2. Singers—Latin America–Biography—Juvenile literature. I. Title.
  ML3930.S46W53 2011
  782.42164092—dc22
  [B]

                                          2010003459

Manufactured in the United States of America

CPSIA Compliance Information: Batch #WS10PK: For Further Information contact Rosen Publishing, New York, New York at 1-800-237-9932

CONTENTS

If you ever listen to the radio, you have likely heard music by Shakira. She has recorded more than eight **albums**. She has also won many awards for her music. She

Here Shakira sings at the MTV Europe Music Awards in Germany.

is not busy only with her music, though. She is also known for her **charity** work. Shakira is a Latin American superstar!

Shakira Isabel Mebarak Ripoll was born in Baranquilla, Colombia, on February 2, 1977. Her father, William Mebarak Chadid, comes from a Lebanese family. He was born in New

Shakira's parents, shown here, are very proud of their daughter's hard work and success.

York but moved to Baranquilla as a baby. Her mother, Nidia Ripoll Torrado, was born in Baranquilla. Shakira's name means "full of grace" or "grateful."

Shakira went to **Catholic** school as a girl. She learned to read, write, and do math there. She also learned to sing and dance. This **education** did not happen in school,

Shakira says that she always knew she would be a singer and songwriter, even when she was young.

Shakira has loved belly dancing since she was a child. She still uses it in her shows.

though. She showed her skill as a dancer at age seven. She jumped up and danced with a group of belly dancers at a Middle Eastern restaurant.

Shakira recorded her first album at age 14. It did not sell very well. She kept trying, though. Her second album sold a little better, but Shakira was not happy. She felt that her first two

Shakira is in the studio recording a song here.

recordings did not
show who she was.
Instead they showed
who her producers
thought she should
be. She decided to
change that in her
next album.

Shakira finished high school before putting out another record. In 1995, *Pies Descalzos* came out. It was a hit! This album sold four million copies in Latin

Here Shakira sings at the 2006 Latin Grammy Awards.

Shakira honors her Latino and Arab roots in her songs.

America. The stage was set for Shakira to gain even more fame. Her next album, *¿Donde están los ladrones?*, won fans in France, Switzerland, Canada, and the United States.

Shakira decided to try making an album in English. *Laundry Service* came out in 2001 and sold more than 13 million copies. She was now a worldwide star! Her next

Shakira sang to a huge crowd in Mexico City. She has a lot of fans!

One of Shakira's 2005 albums was in Spanish, and the other album was in English.

two albums did just as well. They both came out in 2005. Once again, her songs topped U.S. and Latin American music charts.

Shakira has done very well in her musical **career**. She wanted to give something back to her community. She started the Pies Descalzos **Foundation** in 1995. This

Shakira is shown here at the opening of one of the six schools started by Pies Descalzos since 2003.

Shakira started a U.S.-based charity in 2008. She reads to one of the U.S. schools that takes part here.

foundation works to make sure poor children can get a good education and healthy food. It opened its first school in 2003, in Quibdó, Colombia.

Shakira has worked hard for education and the poor. In 2003, UNICEF made Shakira a goodwill **ambassador**. She is the youngest

In December 2007, Shakira visited a school in Teghor, Bangladesh, as part of her work with UNICEF.

Here Shakira takes a walk with children who go to a UNICEF school in Rhajshahi, Bangladesh.

person to have served in this job. UNICEF works to make the lives of children better around the world. Shakira has gone to such countries as Spain, El Salvador, and Bangladesh for UNICEF.

Shakira is shown here reading with children during her visit to Bangladesh.

19

Shakira has won many awards for her music and her charity work. She has also been honored with Grammy Awards in the United States and Latin America. She has won many MTV Video

In 2009, Shakira won two awards at the 40 Principales (Top 40) Awards in Spain.

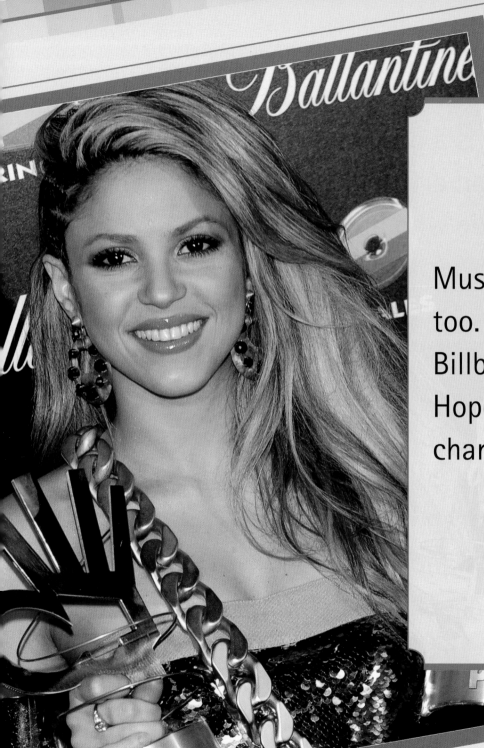

Music Awards,
too. She won the
Billboard Spirit of
Hope Award for her
charity work.

Shakira helped found ALAS in 2006. This is a group of Latin American artists and businesspeople who are working together to make

early childhood education better in Latin American countries. She came out with another album in 2009, called *She Wolf*. There is sure to be more to come from this star singer!

GLOSSARY

albums (AL-bumz) Recordings or groups of songs.

ambassador (am-BA-suh-dur) Someone who is the voice for a country or group and who visits another country or group to share a message.

career (kuh-REER) A job.

Catholic (KATH-lik) Of the Roman Catholic faith.

charity (CHER-uh-tee) Giving to help the needy.

education (eh-juh-KAY-shun) Schooling or training.

foundation (fown-DAY-shun) A group set up to give help for a cause.

INDEX

WEB SITES

Due to the changing nature of Internet links, PowerKids Press has developed an online list of Web sites related to the subject of this book. This site is updated regularly. Please use this link to access the list: www.powerkidslinks.com/hh/shakira/